Poems of Pure Love for Life

127 POEMS TO ENJOY

DR. SHERRI LYNN BURES

Order this book online at www.trafford.com
or email orders@trafford.com

Most Trafford titles are also available at major online book retailers.

Printed in the United States of America.

ISBN: 978-1-4907-3125-4 (sc)
ISBN: 978-1-4907-3127-8 (hc)
ISBN: 978-1-4907-3126-1 (e)

Library of Congress Control Number: 2014905278

Trafford rev. 03/24/2014

 www.trafford.com

North America & international
toll-free: 1 888 232 4444 (USA & Canada)
fax: 812 355 4082

Love is vast beyond wisdom . . .
Love is unconditional . . .
Love is a gift from God . . .

Dedication

To God-Thank you and I am grateful for all of my blessings
To Jesus, the Holy Spirit, Mother Mary, Mary Magdalene, St. Theresa, St.
Michael, St. Jude, my #1 Soldier, and all of my angels, spirits, and guides
To my dear friend Hattie who encouraged me, God Bless always
To my children-Dr. Paul, Suzy, Robert, and Mickey, I love you
To my dear friends Debby, Judy, and Terry
To Grandma Eva Mám tě ráda
To my daughter Suzy and Steve, whose hands introduced
me to the beautiful language of The Deaf Community
To the men and their families in the Ist Battalion, 2nd Marines. Thank you.
To the one who holds my heart, I will love you always
May God Bless all of you and May God Bless each one of you reading
this book, and everyone that you also hold dear to your hearts . . .

Contents

A Perfect Rose

A perfect rose you gave to me,
    Pledge I did my love, to thee . . .
Its bloom it was both white and pink,
    I glanced over and saw you blink . . .
We both knew the love we did share,
    We made such a perfect pair . . .
The fragrance did last one whole week,
    Never did I miss a chance to peek . . .
So beautiful the rose still in my room,
    Reminding me of you, my heart does zoom . . .
Thank you for my sweetest rose,
    Giving it to me, I gave you a special pose . . .
I will tuck it in my Bible someday,
    Dreaming of you, that I may . . .
Cherishing all that you have done,
    You're my love, my sweetheart, my fun . . .
A rose you did give me, and I do adore,
    Your love continues to grow, it shall soar . . .

A Special Place to Stay

Tucked in a special place, deep within my sheltered heart,
I see my love, as he lay next to me.
You touch me softly, as I respond you say,
Tuck me in a special place to stay.

You loved me whole, as no one has done,
Wild imaginations of beings we did yield too.
Causing you stillness, not till day would break,
Tuck me in a special place to stay.

Love making surreal, such pleasure it gave,
Deep feelings, alive they did burst to hear.
Wholeness I felt, knowing completely of him,
Tuck me in a special place to stay.

When memories fade, as the leaves start to fall,
And conversations no longer, go hourly into the night.
Then you will remember a time, you did say, as did I,
Tuck me in a special place to stay.

And when we are older, to old to recall,
Our thoughts are mixed up, all over the wall.
Our hearts still will be strong, and they will release,
That special place you tucked me in, your heart, to keep!!!

A Wish from the Heart

Needing you now as time has settled in,
Confessions of my soul, aching to release,
Intuitiveness you had, yet silent your tongue,
Allowing time to expel silence . . .
Masquerading truths hard to bare,
Channels of thoughts,
Hiding hurt for you not to despair . . .
Emotions buried deep silenced by a façade of calmness,
Appearing you released my heart from captivity,
Knowing compassions,
Flowing swiftly from your heart . . .
Joining its own, balancing its whole,
Intertwined they manage,
To rationalize this world,
Knowledge is known,
As emotions attain freedom,
You accept, you understand,
Truth is here,
For our hearts cannot divide,
Wholeness shall be complete,
It is Given,
He knows all,
He is forever mine . . .

All That I Am

All that I am,
All that I want to be,
All of my love I give to you,
Freely and securely with nothing to ask,
Accepting all of this,
Because you just know,
What truth is at last,
Saying nothing at all,
From distances far away,
Yet knowing how deeply,
My love is here to stay,
I treasure all thoughts,
Of you as they pass my way,
Memorizing your face,
As it shines so to say,
My sweetheart I'm yours,
Forever as you know,
Acceptance of this truth,
Is known unto you,
So treasure it dearly,
Hold it always in your heart,
And strength shall it surface,
To help us, as we are apart,
Our love will survive,
For surely it will,
For all of your thoughts,
Darling, I surely fulfill . . .

And He Looked

And he looked, as if he needed to touch,
 That girl, he loved oh so very much . . .
So shy she appeared, as if to say,
 Come let's be friends, forever our own way . . .
His tiny foot tingled upon the top of her shoe,
 At last he had crossed the line, please she said do . . .
And he reached so gently on her cheek,
 Pushing her closer to him, she was so weak . . .
She fell into his arms and melted away,
 Forgot where she was, for over a day . . .
And he kissed so gentle, yet so pure,
 He now would become her only cure . . .
And he said, I found you
 I want you
 I got you
 I love you
And she said, I want you
 I hoped for you,
 I am holding you,
 I love you . . .

And She Knew

And she knew she would love him,
    From the very start,
    He was the only man,
    She had ever given her heart . . .
And he fantasized of how,
    She would look as a lass,
    So beautiful dressed in white,
    She could have been kept under glass . . .
And the roses fell down,
    By her feet, they did lay,
    Wishing her peace, contentment, and joy,
    On this beautiful day . . .
And white babies breath,
    Adorned her beautiful crown,
    A precious sweet smile,
    That never would see a frown . . .
And dressed in white,
    This angel he saw,
    He knew his love,
    Must be legalized by law . . .
And she looked so innocent,
    Except with her eyes, he knew,
    She had a plan for him,
    Those eyes gave the clue . . .
And her childish ways,
    Melted him right into her,

He knew he longed to be with her,
 There was no cure . . .
And her breath would whisper,
 I love you to him,
 His sensual feelings he knew,
 Was more than a whim . . .
And the feel when you know,
 Your knees will tumble,
 As soon as your sweetheart,
 He does yet mumble . . .
And you know in your heart,
 You don't need to set a date,
 She is forever in your heart,
 Truly it is your fate . . .
And those three little words,
 She says to you,
 Letting you know,
 She'd surely say I do . . .
And the look,
 Of how she was as a lass,
 In your mind, you would never,
 Never, ever let it pass . . .
And the innocence would melt,
 The two into one,
 That look in her eyes,
 Would tell you she won . . .

And She Wrote Love Poems, Just Because

And she wrote love poems, just because,
He was never out of her thoughts, ever,
Encompassing her every emotion, his soul remained,
Attached deep inside at the core of her being,
Content that their souls intertwined,
Poetic justice would service swiftly,
Carrying her off to distant planes of existence,
Where neither would ever part,
And the words comforted her,
When no one else could,
Blossoming her feelings of love, as they should,
Coming at times unknown, only to God,
Flourishing deep affections with her—one,
So she wrote, emotions tumbling,
Over paper so white,
Describing patterns of light, illuminating feelings,
And through her words she knew,
His heart was lit, and sensations would never shatter,
Just service to perfect love, and never quit . . .

And You Hope

And you hope,
    Above hope,
    That he too understands,
    What love is about—
Love is not always gracious,
    Allowing us, too—but love,
It is testing,
    Our patience, our courage, our strength,
It is not for the mere meek,
For it entails trust,
    And above that truth,
That when you gave your heart,
When you told God, you did love,
    With your total being,
When you did share,
    Love stretching into commitment,
As we also said our truth, to God,
    On a midsummer night,
We would honor each other,
    And if there were tribulations,
Follow our heart,
    Back to the one,
    The one, true one that holds the key . . .

As I Lay Down to Sleep

As I lay down to sleep,
    Did I not feel, my love, come to me,
Surrendering my whole,
    Sweat pouring from inside,
    Burning so deep,
I couldn't comprehend,
    Giving way to expressions of love,
    My man was here,
He was pleasuring me,
    Pleasing me beyond belief,
My perfect creation,
    For my heart's indulgence,
Cascading emotions traveling through this night,
Never alone, complete fulfillment,
Powerlessness with bursts of white-
    Rockets propelling upwards,
    Into the heavens,
    Where realities are our dreams,
    Our desires, our true selves,
And he is mine,
    As I am his,
For traveling there,
    Safe, secure,
We are together,
    As our hopes-desire us to be,
Perfectly achieving,
My femininity in his manliness,
    Let me stay,
And ponder, forever,
    My love in his as such,
This is how-I shall live . . .

As No One Else Could

You touched me sweetheart,
  As no one else could,
Your love let me embrace, and
  Hold it so dear to remember,
The truth of your quiet words,
The wisdom of the thoughts you have,
The kindness of your heart
Your loyalty to those you love
There can be no other,
In this world or another,
That has brought such blessings and hope
My sweetheart, how can I ever forget,
You touched me deeply, as no one else could.

Bits of Confusion

Bits of confusion,
    Pieces of the puzzle . . .
Resolving itself into,
    A manifold of knowing-
Truth-all that is-
Confirmation given to us,
Re-exams the realms of happenings,
Now and possibly to come,
Love so unreal,
Wonderful as it can be,
Releases these chains on me . . .
To experience Glory,
So beautiful, heaven,
I have seen it could be . . .

Caress in the Moonlight

Caresses in the moonlight,
   Thoughts of you, to my delight . . .
So grand I remember,
   Way back the month after September . . .
When your arms engulfed me,
   As the moon and stars we would see . . .
And whisper did you,
   Of love so beautiful and true . . .
That I await, our next week, fate,
   Love shall surround myself, my mate . . .
Blossoming inward until it will burst,
   Causing nothing but wishing you first . . .
And moonlit strolls shall enhance the feel,
   Causing sensuous feelings, oh so real . . .
Trying to control all the emotion I have,
   Enjoying moments with you, my fav . . .
Holding you gently, memorizing the night,
   Never letting go, till the dawn, it will light . . .
But memories we shall make, for a lifetime to last,
   Our time together, runs to fast . . .
I love you now, more than ever before,
   You my darling, feel my whole core . . .

Come to Me Quickly

Come to me quickly sweetheart,
Satisfy this craving for love,
Never ceasing to exist,
Always calmly tantalizing me,
As sunset it surrenders,
I anticipate calling to you,
Secretly holding my heart,
Whispering the sweetest of names,
Ease this longing-Sweetheart,
Bubbling constantly, yearning to pleasure you,
Contemplating this day is over,
Calling outward, come quickly at last,
My heart feels exhausted, anticipating bliss,
Sweetheart, will you always be mine,
Though I never need wonder,
For certainty echoes in my mind,
Entering forcefully, totally engulfing my being,
Raging through all dimensions,
Until total acceptance is achieved, and
Yearning deeply begins anew,
Anticipating of yet another tomorrow,
When my sweetheart, will come again, at last . . .

Come to Me Sweetheart

Come to me sweetheart,
    Filling my heart with delight . . .
Let me feel my hearts pulsations,
    As only you can do it right . . .
Deeply you, arriving to the end,
    Portions of me, never entered before . . .
Come alive with the power,
    You have restored . . .
Gentleness will surround me,
    This newborn morn,
And take me to new heights,
    I've longed for ecstatically,
For, at last, you have come,
And filtered love, throughout
    This passionate body,
    That dwells in your heart,
    And throughout . . .
As this love will carry us through,
    Each passing hour,
    That we shall-have to go . . .
Allowing us courage, strength, and
    Substance to grow . . .
And forever, just be . . .

The kindness that I need,
    For kindness was what,
      Brought this tender heart to me . . .
Such kindness never seen,
    In perfect politeness a being . . .
Such supreme divine,
    Our love is interconnected,
    And as this day unfolds . . .
As surely as it must,
Clings, I will to the trust,
    I've found in his true being . . .
Allowing me the sanctionary,
    To be the woman I am . . .
Allowing me to be my all,
    Only asking to hold my hand . . .
Our love will be complete,
    As our Lord, will see as such . . .
Encircling our visions,
    Enriching our lives, ever so much . . .
Living our life so full, so full . . .

Come to Me While the Light is Still Dim

Come to me while the light is still dim,
    For to your woman-bestow her every whim,
While the breath of dawn is young,
    Bring to her, your harvest, for to her it is just begun,
Mellowing into the sweetness that lays below,
    Indulge your pleasures, bring about your glow,
Fly with a dove that cascades you adieu,
    To a magical hideaway meant for but few,
That island you love far in a distant land,
    Tenderly melt into her being, simply by touching her hand,
Conveying your everlasting love to her,
    For her deep centered emotions cause her to purr,
And rescue her slightly as the dusk haze fades away,
    Promise your Sweetheart, return nightly to your bay,
Now bring her back slowly to her earthly work she must,
    For the peace she has found, was from her man's lust,
We both will continue to escape, every chance to that place,
    For my angel loves to touch me, and embrace my face . . .

Darling, I Know You are Here

Darling, I know you are here,
When I close my eyes,
I drift softly away,
Somewhere you can only touch me,
You know how,
Swirling me faster and faster,
    We go upwards,
Where visions of sunset colors,
    Dance through my head,
Where feelings pulse down,
    While I sit on my bed,
Knowing you're touching-
    So intense, I can feel,
I try to send you, messages of love,
So kind,
I try to send them, to tell you-you are mine,
Channeling energy,
Along crisscrossed highways-
To your heart,
Knowing only my love,
    Will get you to start,
You have connected with me,
    As you do through the day,

Our own special feelings,
　　We decide when to say,
Our Lord made it possible,
　　For us this way,
To reassure each other,
　　Of our presence throughout the day,
Love, I close my eyes,
　　As I sense you so near,
Sending love to you,
　　Because you are so dear,
Then back to my work,
　　That I must somehow do,
Don't worry my darling,
　　I will again-love you,
For you can always contact me,
You come inside of me,
　　And settle in your cozy place,
　　To take good care of me,
You know what triggers everyone,
　　Of my favorite spots . . .

Dimensions We Share

Closeness, I feel as you cascade down inside me,
  Pulsating my every breath,
  Though you are far,
Your breath comes to me,
  Echoing down my throat,
  My lips close, to hold you inward,
We are together,
  Dimensions have opened,
  You are in my arms,
Oh, what thoughts escalate this body,
  What temptuous desires I crave,
Yes, you obey, as my Lover,
You know-
  Without one whisper, that I have spoken,
You know, oh, what magic you instill,
  Until daybreak appears,
  And I must go,
  Unto the harsh realities of this world,
Away, from a dimension that we both share,
A time and place, precious,
  For we are together,
  And no one, and no amount of distance,
  Can eliminate me from those arms,
  I love to hold,
  And escape with my soul,
Into—Dimensions We Share . . .

Emotional Level
of Unconscious Bliss

Experiencing such an emotional level of unconscious bliss,
I wander aimlessly back to this reality,
Overwhelmed from rainbow of colors vanishing into another,
Masquerading whispers of angels floating by,
Birds chanting to each other, yet distinctly hearing each call,
To another-as if they are reciting our song,
Layers upon layers revealing depths I have never perceived before,
Christ revealed,
I could not foresee,
For the richness that has been endowed upon me,
Was revaluated to me,
As if I walked through heaven's gate,
And unimaginable sensations of Glory hit upon me,
Clarity was revealed-meaning of Love-
Unselfish acts of my love revealed,
Through my joy-he too has found joy,
Inspiring words meant only for him,

Sent to him as though total passion enlightening,
Words revealed for his betterment,
Content-yet a peace enriched,
That I have fallen once more,
Yet deep I have fallen,
Into his magical arms of delight,
That I have dreamed of,
Known-Yet-not known,
But spilled together, united as one,
For a force, just so powerfully true,
To bring forth to me,
Anytime I think of you,
Sweetheart, it is you,
As long as I live,
You have given me a honeymoon-
From your heart,
That sends me from here until the moon . . .

Enough-You Are

Enough-
You are,
Never ask,
Just accept,
Enough-
I'm sure,
So perfect,
Your smile,
Your total sense,
Of Love,
Enough-
Yes,
Its truth,
The T you told me,
Enough-
My love,
Always
And one day . . .

For the One

For the one that makes her life, oh, so grand,
    With just one swirl, the touch of his hand . . .
She looked at the face, so perfect in her mind,
    As he came closer, oh he is so kind, so kind . . .
Roses for her, always did he bring,
    With passion only for him, her voice shall soon sing . . .
Oh the blessings from above, she has her boy,
    Leaning ever so closer, he too, has his toy . . .
A gentleman he shall, one day become,
    For he waits for his lass, not as some . . .
He just takes a look, and he knows deep within,
    How possibly could he ever be without her, his Lynn . . .
So the happiest to both, on this day,
    Each loves the other, in a unique, but special way . . .

Gazing Quietly

Gazing quietly unto the acres of evergreens,
I close my eyes, longing for the wonderment of you,
Swirling deep inside, as the wind-love comes,
Exploding my senses, into joining each other,
As if it had always been,
None had ever known-the other did not exist . . .
They were Home-Comfortable,
Delighted to combine into a harmony of transitional lights,
Hues of pinks and lavenders,
Caressing my body, sensing your presence so deep,
Carrying me into level upon level of imaginary wonders,
Unknown until this man, fulfilled my void,
Love hath appeared,
And danced into my heart,
Escaping all rhyme and reason,
Releasing my inhibitions unto him,
Raising my subconscious to levels,
Unimaginable to ever speak of-
I am in you, feeling your heart beating,
I sense all that you are,
We are as one together . . .
Auras of pinks and lavenders,
Appearing before me,
Transmitting me into a sense of completeness . . .
   I am his . . .
   I want no other . . .
   He is my all . . .
All that I want is now known . . .
This place, this man, this feeling of love . . .
So divine, known to us both,
Serenity, Peace, My Equal, My Man, My All . . .

Written about the evergreen trees in the Brecksville
Metro-parks in Cleveland, Ohio

41

Happy New Year, Darling

My love you are the kindest man that I know,
    It was that trait that brought me to you, so . . .
I knew the first day we met,
    A friend I could depend on, I bet . . .
Your smile illuminated my heart at first,
    Your kindness touched me, as I burst . . .
The angels sent you to me, for me to enjoy,
    They knew I needed that kind of boy . . .
Our connection it grew stronger everyday,
    Our love and friendship, we do it our way . . .
So Happy New Year darling, I love you so,
    Two hearts are one, and together shall we go . . .

Hearts Colliding

Hearts colliding blissful, unto one another,
Familiarity so surreal-They melt,
Into a perfect concoction of-
Thoughts, wishes, hopes and desires,
Purity at its finest,
Riveted down from the heavens,
Uniting as into a web,
Not destructible-unapproachable,
Because blessed by the purest of forms, we know,
Existence satisfies our every whim,
Questions are answered, no more to ponder,
My heart had been reunited,
With its lost piece,
Allowing it to master itself into a
Grace of stunning purity,
And expressing love so profound,
Only my hearts equal can it be known . . .

Hearts Melt Into One

Hearts melted into one,
Forgetting how to breathe,
I whisper to you,
Gently kissing away the distances,
Erased from our perception of reality,
Unwilling to sacrifice,
Releasing yet again and again,
Not accepting to forfeit all desires,
This force-engulfs me-powerfully-
Trembling me-I gasp . . .
Deepens and deepens it grows,
Into a massive motion of love,
That he and I alone can make . . .
Enjoy, indulge, Oh!
I can't control the passions,
Oh, God, I scream . . . I love him,
How, how, can he feed my soul,
Carry me through the night,
The day, my everything,
Everything escapes me,
Except this yearning for him,
Releasing myself into his heart,
I feel whole,
So perfect, I am at peace, I am calm,
I sleep with him,
My love, my man, the one . . .

How Do You Know

How do you know?
How do you know, just how to touch me,
That I quiver all over,
How do you know, to stroke me from top to bottom,
As the Duchess of Dover . . .
How do you know, when I need to hear-
Your voice, so calm,
How do you know, when making love to me,
And then softly touch my palm . . .
How do you know, to satisfy-
Your woman beyond control,
How do you know, every inch to touch,
From her forehead to sole . . .
How do you know, all through the day,
Sending signals you adore,
How do you know, she's the one,
Everything you wished for . . .
How do you know, every dreamy way,
You tell her good night,
How do you know, you send her love,
Even if you're not in sight . . .
You, my love, just do,
You just do . . .

I Found So Much Peace

I found so much peace and contentment, my love,
Surrounding my soul, savoring up to the heavens,
Whirls of love surrounding our hearts,
As my breath sweetly, heard inside you,
Essences exchanged, challenging our spirits,
All knowledge exchanged, as peace abounds,
Everlasting love acknowledged,
With whirls and whirls of beautiful lights,
Love spread so completely, with nothing left undone,
Always forever, as it never fades . . .

I Knew When You Came to Me

Yes, I knew when you came to me,
Because I know how much you care,
Forcefully arriving before dawn,
I awakened to a large thrust,
Happily accepting, this gift of love, so real . . .
Exhilarated to begin again, a new day . . .
Adventure awaits us both,
Yet, now we are together,
As all was intended,
Serene-renewed . . .
Blessed to know you, the one . . .
My dreams turn to realities with,
Sweetness at its finest,
I await for one more encounter,
With my beloved, Sweetheart . . .
For I know in my heart,
It will be, it will be . . .

I Need to Speak

I need to speak,
To hear your voice,
Endless are these moments,
Away from you,
For more than a time,
Wondering where we shall share,
Each other again,
I'm not strong, yet I try,
Try for all the reasons you do,
Because I know, I should,
Give it to God,
To determine what shall be,
For he alone-knows all,
And who am I to ask,
So I sit, starring at the sky,
Outside, wondering if you too,
Are thinking of me,
Let it be, yes, let it be . . .

I Study Your Face

I study your face, while you lay softly next to me,
Gazing at your beautiful eyes, drawing me to them,
We caress, softly, gently, stroking me with whispers of delight,
Until my emotions explode, he is mine, I am complete,
For to know of this love, I need no other,
Fulfilling and sweet, whispering songs of our longings-past,
Yet, jetting me into this time, this universe, my being,
And with a gentle touch, of his hand,
I lose reality,
Gasping-take all of me, do all you can,
For such fulfillment, have I not known,
And this longing of lust,
Reaches out to greet me,
Expanding my horizons, searching my soul,
For that puzzle piece-it is you,
My perfect desire has been met,
With one sweep of his touch across my breast,
And the feel of him,
Pulling me closer to feelings, so surreal,
Pleasurable to both he and I . . .
You have been,
Always will be,
It is . . .

I Will Follow The Stars to Your Heart

I will follow the stars to your heart,
Gazing the galaxy, never to part . . .
Love so deep, it will glow,
Whether down south, or in the snow . . .
I cuddle next to you, as I go to sleep,
You'll never hear a word from me, not a peep . . .
For to sleep next to you, you touch me so sweet,
I hear, for I do listen, my heart does skip a beat . . .
It longs to be near you, have you by its side,
As I drift off to sleep, gently feeling your tide . . .
You caress me yet closer, so close my dear,
Remembering to erase my one tear, my one fear . . .
You give me my strength, to cope, with such hope,
Loving me so deeply, forgetting I did ever mope . . .
My time turns to dreams, it is there I do gaze,
My love hath arrived, I see him in the haze . . .
Dreams are consumed with my sweet for a while,
We have traveled so far, perhaps now down the Nile . . .
For our passions do send me, places still,
I love to go there; my angel will give me a chill . . .

In The Calm of The Day

A beautiful peace, came softly to me,
In this calm of the day . . .
Blissfully unknown,
Movement of soft flutters,
Slowly move inward . . .
Reaching centers, yearning to burst open,
Awaiting yet a signal to spark,
Ignite to passion . . .
Circling my senses,
Awaiting to be reunited,
With this sense . . .
Overpowering my will,
Love has come,
Yet again . . .
Surprising me,
Yet, charming its cast always . . .
Welcoming joy,
For to deny,
I might regret . . .
Glorious, as it came,
It leaves its mark . . .
A love cast upon me,
In this calm of the day,
To enrich me,
Fill me,
And remind me . . .
Love cometh-
When it decides,
And accepting,
Is so blessed . . .
For we are truly blessed,
To have found it . . .
Rare in its kind,
Magnificence,
In its Love,
And truly leaving us always,
In its Awe . . .

Let Me Give You a Hug

Let me give you a hug for all of time . . .
For time no one has given us enough of . . .
The moments they are, but precious and few . . .
I capture them all, alas but a few . . .

Let me give you a hug for all of time . . .
To capture that feeling oh so divine . . .
It encompasses my soul . . .
And carries me off, alas but to you . . .

Let me give you a hug for all of time . . .
To still this heart, though it beats oh so fine . . .
And fill me with love oh so pure . . .
To carry me away, for this I am sure . . .

Let Me Show You

Let me show you, how much I care,
From every breath we take, to every moment we share,
Hold me so close, as though all my yesterdays,
Melt into just today,
Caress every piece of me,
Envelope my total being into you,
As we become one,
Lose our inner beings,
To this magnificence of just being,
Pounding each pulse point,
Dancing us into total bliss,
Unending, never escaping back into reality,
This total empowerment, strengthens, and nourishes us,
Magnifying us to believing we,
Can conquer problems to vast to exist,
Sealing our destiny into,
A universe unknown to exist,
Yet contemplating perhaps another time,
Our body's sensory points go,
Beyond our imagination,
Controlling deeply, bursting with such pleasures,
Longing to be released, back into our creativity,
To prosper us, make us strong, and know-
My life force is you . . .

Let Me Write as a Child

Let me write as a child,
　　Let my imagination go wild . . .
To be as free as you can,
　　Not restricted as a woman or man . . .
To write straight from your heart,
　　With not an ending, just a start . . .
To be as honest, innocent, and kind,
　　Letting all thoughts float from your mind . . .
Take me back to that innocent time,
　　When everything cost a nickel or a dime . . .
When television was still black and white,
　　And all the colors of the rainbow, oh so bright . . .
Ice cream cones were a pure delight,
　　And racing through the park, flying your kite . . .
A, B, C's were still not an ordinary thing,
　　And I could hear Michael Jackson and sing . . .
Take me back to a time back then,
　　When I was perhaps nine or ten . . .
And follow me everyday of your life,
　　And when we become adults, I'll be your wife . . .

Look At My Soldier

Look at my soldier-
Look towards that man-
   That lay quietly at rest,
Pondering not-the fields of war,
   Yet to come,
Yet, I do-
   I ponder,
   I pray,
Quietly-not for his ears to hear,
   My fears, overshadowed,
With the purest scent of Divine Light and Love,
Forgetting not-
   Yet cherishing,
Casting this moment into my heart, my core,
For he is safe-
   Now the present-
Where will he yet go-
   What missions what he might face-
Will this gentlest of times, remain in him-
To bring him calm, serenity, peace,
It is not for me to understand-
   Our Creator knows all,

And we-those who remain safe,
　　Guarded in our world of certainty-
Must allow them,
　　The freedom to act,
　　Act in ways for our better protection,
And remembering that feel-
　　Of when he slept,
　　My soldier dear,
Was at the calmest of peace,
Knowing-love was near,
And this one moment in time,
　　This precious moment,
　　Caressed in both our hearts-
Would carry us into the trials of tomorrow,
And the blessedness of a reunion-foreseen . . .

Dedicated to my son Lt. Commander Sir Paul Bures and
the 1st Battalion, 2nd Marines and their families

Look Into The Sky

Look into the sky-
    Of blue and white,
Cuddles of clouds,
    Broken by sky below,
Horizons of blue,
    Touching as if I-
    See the ocean touching,
    The sky at night,
Seeing God's creation of glory,
    He knows all,
    And has all the answers,
I ponder mine,
    Not knowing when I should,
    Have you in my arms,
Tops of clouds,
    Freely sitting,
    Yet moving,
Slowly from your eye to mine,
And your soul and mine,
    Dance upon these clouds,
    Someday,
When we are free,
    To choose our destiny,
Searching the tops of the clouds,
    Feeling your closeness,
I wait to hear your-
Precious word,
From the one that holds
My heart . . .

Look Up at The Moon

Look up at the moon, and see our glimmering light,
Illuminating the sky, oh so beautiful this night . . .
From a far off galaxy, did you once decide to appear,
To be my shining angel, and my one Sweetheart, so dear . . .
Giving my heart hope, much more than a trace,
You have traveled far in this galaxy, for my face . . .
For it welcomes to you, its open mind and heart,
Succumbing its security, it felt cupids dart . . .
And my world from that day would change,
It knew your existence, and would need to arrange . . .
For look only up, to the moon and the sun,
And my love you will see where our love had begun . . .
It was long ago and very far away,
Distant lands had already, taken my heart a sway . . .
You had it then, and gave it back to me for a while,
You would walk heaven and earth to find me, more than a mile . . .
My heart it did have all its desire and passion back,
It would never be again lonely, nor would love ever it lack . . .

Love is Something You Can Never Predict

Love is something you can never predict,
It springs upon you suddenly . . .
Emerging itself on a once stable place,
Complicating yet completing itself . . .
Filling dreams of perfectness,
Questioning disappears with an unreal acceptance . . .
Inexperienced, up unto this time,
My darling with you . . .

Make Love to Me Slowly

Make love to me slowly, tenderly this night,
    Let me hold you so freely, I'll see the light . . .
For I'm bursting so full, I need you to hold,
    Swirling deep penetrations, my love, I've been told . . .
Sensations so wild, trying to concentrate during the day,
    Dreaming of you fulfilling me, as I lay . . .
Soon you will be, my love, in my arms,
    Sheltering me from this world, ending the harms . . .
And as you penetrate me deeply, the sensations I shall feel,
    Moments that will last my lifetime, sometimes so surreal . . .
Lifting me upwards, to the heavens shall we soar,
    Begging you to go onward, screaming I want more . . .
Trusting you completely, your love will always be,
    Fresh and satisfying, always surrounding me . . .

Make Love to Me Tenderly

Make love to me tenderly,
Carry me through this darkened night,
Whisper thoughts of love so pure,
That only you may possess my heart,
Banish all thoughts of betrayal that seeks in,
Negativity surrounded with a tempestuous cloud,
Ponder not of jealousy,
For it darkens the light that glows on us,
Love me as your princess,
Let me adore you as my prince,
Wild thoughts and desires so clear,
That we might take yet some,
Bury them deep within the trenches of our beings,
And bring them yet forth,
When our love is questioned,
For to unbury the treasure,
Will bring peace to a questioning mind,
Make love to your temple,
Treat her with sweetness so kind,
That love will encircle its magic,
Captivating our souls,
And nourishing us back,
Into the oneness we savor,
And hold as our own-
Our truth-our Love . . .

Make Love to Me All Through The Night

Make love to me, all through the night,
  Caress me gently, and hold me so tight . . .
Soar me off to wonderland, never letting go,
  Giving me the chance to never say no . . .
Fill me with your being, as you only can,
  Satisfy all my desires, my sweet, sweet man . . .
I love you angel always, you I adore,
  I'll whisper sweet thoughts to you, give me more . . .
You are my special sweetheart, as I belong to you,
  Make this moment magically multiply by two . . .

Makes Me Complete

You made love to me, this morning,
So passionate, so true-
Tenderly banishing traces of tears, from my eyes,
You knew-you knew-
This love would carry me,
For distances we dare not know,
I look in wonderment, where are you now,
High above me in the clouds you soar,
Taking you back to places so familiar to you before,
Yet, it is here you wish to be,
In my arms, you crave to embrace,
So secure and serene,
All of you, is complete in this world,
Where I dwell . . .
Where eagles do soar, that is where,
The nearness of you remains,
I close door upon door,
Searching for my love once more,
My love-I seek, your beautiful brown eyes,
Yet, you are gone-it is no surprise,
When shall you return,
I dare not know,
Yet, passion will bring us together again-
It is he I seek,
It is he that makes me complete . . .

Mesmerize Me

Mesmerize me-
Challenge my soul to go deeper inside yours-
   Whirl me inside, where none has been,
Explore all possibilities-
   As we glide forward,
   Hand in hand,
Colliding now, into a perfect transgression
   Of one realm to another,
   Where our deepest fantasies,
   Are alive,
   And we have found peace,
Hearts have melted,
   You are totally engulfed in me,
   As we descend yet further,
Exploring our home, our tranquility,
   Where peace and contentment,
   Lie within our grasp,
At that one perfect time,
   In a galaxy of dreams,
   We have dreamt,
Ours transpires us to distances erased,
   Where our past and present collide,
   We become one,
Perfect, sexual, our knowledge of this,
   Given to us from our Lord-
To perfect our love-
   Into an unending chemistry of just being,
   Serene, unpretentious,
Deserving-we accept,
For this time has given us this chance,
   To be as we were before,
Beautifully sculptured Camelot of lush,
   Sweet tenderness divine,
   Where you and I totally did shine,
And you my love,
   Were totally mine . . .

When Life Seems Settled

When you are looking for love,
You look for love that is like yourself,
You find a love different than yourself,
And then realize you are so alike after all.

You never expect feelings to reappear,
Suddenly come stronger than ever before.

When life seems settled, ideas appear,
New thoughts come and life is,
Rejuvenated, new ways and thoughts appear,
Hopes and dreams are renewed.

And the love you found in the strangest of places,
That took you totally by surprise,
Establishes new life, hope, and joy,
Into what used to be a predictable life . . .

When Life Surprise Us With Love

Love is something, time does not command,
Springing itself suddenly into obsession,
Emerging itself unto a once stable place,
Complicating hearts, yet completing them . . .

Dreaming of love, as I've not seen before,
Finding it, alas so different, so true,
Realizing familiarity abounds between,
Surprising feelings stronger, so beware . . .

Hopes are surfaced, as dreams come alive,
New processes of being, abound so fast,
Perfectness of dreams fulfilled and accepted,
Unexplained, my Sweetheart, until this time . . .

My Angel, My Soldier

He saluted me, not in this world-
    But the next,
Where angels and saints, their love keeps us strong,
He consoled me, my tears never able to finish,
Floodgates opened, waters rushing and raging,
    Uncontrollable, as if lifetimes of knowledge-
Questioning, why this one has to finish,
Timing, is explained,
God's divine wisdom, as only our Maker,
Our Creator can control,
I'll be with you always,
I heard both clear,
    As if a whisper of pure knowledge,
    Satisfied my soul,
Always when you sleep,
    And feel that tender touch upon your cheek,
Always when you go outside,
    And look up toward the sky,
Always when you quietly say your prayers,
    He listens, Always my love and one day,
For eternity comes,
    Oh so fast,
We are here, but to experience this earthly world,
So stay, grow, cherish your time,
And when all is done, on this earthly plane,
I shall meet you at the doors of heaven,
    With open arms, a smile, and radiant peace,
To know-you are home,
And quietly he said,
I am your #1 soldier-
And as he saluted-
For all of Heaven-
    They would all be in Awe . . .

My Beautiful Creation

My perfect creation,
  You lie so close,
    Beneath the clouds, separating us,
My heart flutters and jumps toward you,
  It knows you are near,
And we must be together, not free,
I gaze unto the blue horizon,
  As it touches the endless white clouds,
Contemplating your existence, beneath,
So close, can I not jump,
To be in your arms,
Reunited with joy, and utter delight,
Yet, I fare another day-without you,
Without the heart that needs healing,
From life causalities, and contemplations,
Hoping it will get better,
Yet, no smile adorns this face,
No laughter comes out to hear,
  Just a sadness surrounding me,
Looking, wandering, Accepting-because I must,
And I look downward, capturing what I can,
Hoping to touch, you, someway-
Knowing-you feel me looking down upon you,
Unknowing, the length of our separation,
I wonder if this—Look,
Commits our souls,
As it has our minds . . .

My Beauty, My Truth, My Destiny

My beauty, my truth, my destiny,
You who can take me to places,
I've never climbed,
Where destiny collides,
   With sensuous delights,
And soaring up on clouds,
   Can become a daily occurrence,
   Within your realms,
Magically opening up,
   New escapades of sheer delight,
   Until I screamed inside,
   With tearful songs riveting,
   To burst into consciousness,
And revealing from the heavens,
   Gifts they have given us,
Talents not explored,
   But always known, with you,
Revealing not just to myself,
   But to a New Awakening,
   A spiritual truth,
That not one, but both souls have made . . .

My Darling As You Whisper

My darling as you whisper,
    Tender thoughts to me,
Remember, my heart melts a little bit,
    More each time,
    Into yours,
The sentiments-your voice,
    Instills upon my heart,
Always carries me away,
    To places known only to you,
Where our love is rich,
    And the thought of you,
    Caressing me into the moonlit night,
Excites me with passions,
    Just waiting to burst,
But your tender goodnights,
    Surround me with warmth,
Knowing your thoughts,
    And messages of us,
I'll carry those words,
    Into the next sunrise,
And I'll see your smile,
    As I fall deep asleep,
Where you shall carry me off,
    To be as one with you . . .

My Darling Let Me Hold You

My darling let me hold you,
But just a little different than before,
A hug to take from you, your sorrow,
And give you hope for tomorrow,
To tightly touch all the parts of you,
Erasing negativity, bidding it adieu,
Never allowing this to be the beginning of the end,
Only positive thoughts will I send,
For strong love will heal now,
This I promise, I give you a vow,
To love you always from today until tomorrow,
Let there be no room right now for sorrow,
So my darling let me hold you,
But just a little more than before,
Letting love burst all through your heart,
With happiness and joy, we never will part,
Love will surround you and heal you whole,
You captured my heart-you have captured my soul . . .

My Inner Spirit Awakens When You Touch Me

My inner spirit awakens when you touch me,
Forcing my senses to explode,
    To expand their horizons,
    Unto the unknown,
Where destiny foresees me,
New challenges beckon me to succumb to them,
A full circle emerges,
    As knowledge explodes to the forefront,
Bringing not just understanding,
    But acceptance of beings,
Differences collide as images glide into the light,
The one pure being,
    That we all are a part of,
Return, we must,
    But fragments and fragments,
    Interlocking together, forming a blending,
    Of all parts, all beings,
Of us, our certainty-unknown,
Yet, through you a purpose is seen,
Captivate moments from your touch,
Stimulate not just my outer being,
But move me to possess this knowledge,
This longing to bring our essences together,
And through that process,
Enlighten me, as to our being,
Our way, our truth,
For through the oneness of you,
    For have I not gravitated to understanding,
    The oneness of all, all creation, all life,
    All Love . . .
For it is from love we were created,
And it is love that we will reunite,
With Him who created us . . .

My Love, Where Are You?

My love, where are you?
   I know, yet I ponder,
   I trust, yet I feel,
Knowing how we feel,
   Yet, I miss,
   The soft sound of your whisper,
Making love to me,
   Across the miles,
The smile I feel,
   Not seen, but felt as if beside me,
Where are you?
   My love,
I can not call, for you too need time,
Time to sort,
   Complexities that surround us,
I wonder,
   Do you think of me,
   While talking to another,
For I know, I do,
You are always,
   You remain,
   The one I long to talk too,
   And be with . . .

My Majesty, My Beautiful Man

My angel sent from heaven above,
  The purest soul my true, true love . . .
How can it be you, so far away,
  I miss you so, all through the day . . .
Dream of you, casting others astray,
  Tugging at decisions, would I betray . . .
My dear, dear one whom I adore,
  Take me away—allow me to soar . . .
High unto the heavens, where the birds do sing,
  My beautiful man, whom I do cling . . .
Show me your passion, yet one more time,
  Dance with me darling, I'll pay the dime . . .
Allow me to be the princess that I can,
  Release to me my majesty, my beautiful man . . .

My Soul Has Such Peace

My soul has such peace, after you make love to me,
 You carry my heart, my dreams, my faith,
 Into a new peace, a new awakening,
For two, to be as one,
 A blessed union, not earthly known,
Bits of heaven, as all is known,
Fully extending such joy unto the deepest dimensions,
 That exist, that we are united,
 In this peace, this calm, this serenity,
You have awakened this year,
 To new sources of love,
 Enriching us, to the fullest extent,
And with such peace,
 I surrender myself, to an inner dimension-
 Of total soul, total self,
Through you, reuniting a whole,
 That never was lost, but just at rest,
And awakened with such magnitude,
 That no force can contain it,
And love so real, so perfect, my beginnings-
 Feel so true, that a new year will bring joy,
 Contentment, and love, my love,
Shall the newest of years, be with you . . .

My Sweet Emotion

My sweet emotion, how can you be,
    The only man, meant truly for me . . .
The look when I glance into your face,
    Makes other men, reverse and erase . . .
The sound of your voice, sends chills to me,
    Longing to feel your lips, oh set me free . . .
For your touch, sends me places, I have never known,
    You alone can send me—I surely have flown . . .
Into the horizons our bodies collide,
    Never allowing my emotions to hide . . .
For the truth have I told you,
    So quietly down within, as you do . . .
We long to stay together, if only we knew,
    Perhaps one day, it can be true . . .
Now I wait as you sleep, so softly by my side,
    Waiting for our passions, soon shall collide . . .
And with reuniting force, shall I begin this day,
    Tonight again, my love, with you, shall I lay . . .
Content in your arms, so magical they be,
    You my darling are meant for me . . .
Sleep my love, and as you awake,
    Of your Sweetheart, you may partake . . .
And whisper sweet nothings of love to your dear,
    And she shall whisper I love you, as you lay so near . . .

My Sweetest of Sweets

My sweetest of sweets,
    My softest touch,
You have illuminated me,
    You have enriched my soul,
The man of my dreams,
    The man I am lucky enough to hold,
Come to me quickly,
    Stay with me this night,
Caress every inch of me,
    Caress me and hold me, oh so tight,
For it's you that I wish for,
    For it's you that holds my heart,
Whisper sweet nothings softly to me,
    Whisper we shall never part . . .

My Truth

My truth, my strength, my love,
I close my eyes,
As God connects you to me,
Our sweet Lord of all creation,
Knows of our love,
As I took my heart,
I am overwhelmed,
With the nearness of you,
Your love penetrate me,
Enriching me to fill myself, my love,
Knowing-our Lord has allowed-
Us to be together,
Blessed us with this precious gift,
Of togetherness-
To make us whole,
Fulfilled, grateful,
That we found in one another,
The piece that we needed,
To complete ourselves,
That one special part,
To complete the circle of love,
And thus in turn enrich all,
Those to which we connect . . .

One Flower

Sometimes it takes just one flower to think of him,
    Memorizing his face in the moonlight, oh so dim . . .
To never forget, to absorb his essences into me,
    To shelter me from harm, I allowed his love to protect, and let it be . . .
The soft touch of his finger, on the palm of my hand,
    Turning my body inside out, desiring him to command . . .
Gently moving closer, and whispering messages of love,
    Seductively teasing my senses,
    Whisking me inward, my sweet dove . . .
And as we did sit by the light of the moon,
    You then lay with your woman, until the next noon . . .
Ever so gently and yet letting her know,
    She is the flower that moves you,
    And the sweetness of a newborn doe . . .

One Glance and I Knew

One glance and I knew,
My heart itself a flutter,
You did not look,
You did not speak,
As if silence would harden-
Feelings deep within,
Yet I did look,
I did feel-
Connections too deep,
To just wash asunder,
Your heart not awake,
As in a timeless silence,
Too deep a sleep,
Much needed from emotions,
Which arose too fast,
As I wait-patiently, silently,
By your side,
And yet alone-
Waiting, hoping,
For your heart to catch up-
To mine . . .

One Simple Touch Will

One simple touch will,
    Erase all time-
One simple kiss,
    Will reunite us as before,
One simple look,
    Will start my heart to tremble,
One simple hug,
    Will encircle us to awaken,
One simple whisper,
    Will set me afire,
And all that we choose,
    Will flow swiftly upon us,
Engulfing our senses to pure passion,
And all of our hurts will,
    Swiftly disappear,
    Into an unknown force,
Till we are separated again . . .

One Spiritual Being

Feelings coming over me, as the dark of night,
    Turns slowly into dawn,
Sweetheart awakens me, pleasures me,
    As only he can,
And we turn, into one, one spiritual being,
    Connected into another realm,
    Where he and I,
    Dance-the song of love,
Passion, it exists,
Strong-Knowing-he is my answer,
My way-
    And we turn deeper-
Inward, exploring new horizons of depth,
Feeling, captivating thoughts of tomorrow,
    When we shall together escape this world,
Into one, symbolic form-
    Of unity, of strength,
Our joy, released into our bodies,
Filling them with endless strength,
Remembering his touching words,
    Those precious thoughts of care,
Yielding onward to possess his love,
    His devotion, his deep adoration of my soul,
As I too-his, do also yield too,
And as we both give to each other,
    We don't hold back,
Yet ultimately melt, so perfect,
That truly our Lord and Creator,
    Has given to us, this gift-
    This Love-this one . . .

Our Soldiers

I watch in amazement, that sky so clear,
  Angels of colors appearing,
    Sunday morning blessings of God, so dear . . .
Powerful waves thrusting power upon the land,
  Only power from our Lord, his hand . . .
I look up to those colors, as they unfold,
  Asking why free will Lord, when will I be told . . .
Why so perfect this place, such peace to abide,
  And yet your ocean Lord away,
    There is yet stride . . .
War not forgotten, yet we put it away,
  Letting others face it-their precious last day . . .
Destruction, lost hope, too much to bear,
  Yet to see your majesty here Lord, I sit and I stare . . .
Help me Lord understand,
  Why such destruction does exist,
    And why on this land, there is no such twist . . .
Thank-you Dear God, for America our land,
  But upon our soldiers in Afghanistan,
    Lay upon them-Your Hand . . .

Patiently Waiting

Patiently waiting silence to disappear,
It has a hold on you,
Not allowing divine light and love to appear,
What seems like contentment,
Ravishes through our hearts,
Filling us with endless wonder-
Your thoughts, not under our control,
Speak out your mind,
Thou profound it may be,
Sensor not your words,
Misunderstanding never shall be,
Loosen your lips,
Speak only of the truth,
Clarify your mind,
And silence no more,
May it be our Enemy . . .

Play Me a Song

Play me a song, to sway my heart,
  Send me love letters and flowers, to fill up a cart . . .
Let me remember what we meant, long ago,
  Light up my fire, the way you just know . . .
For I'll ask for all things, for the lover in you,
  Green pastures to run in, try to catch me, under the sky so blue . . .
My gifts to you will be all smiles and giggles,
  Yours to me, will be to see lots of wiggles . . .
I'll ask for it all, from sunrise to sunset,
  A walk under the moonlit stars, surely you can bet . . .
For I have found the man of my dreams,
  I want the whole world, to hear all my screams . . .
So play me a song, yes Sweetheart, do sway my heart,
  Remember I loved you dearly, right from the start . . .

Remember It is You My Love

Remember it is you my love, that starts my heart to quiver,
  Giving of yourself completely to me, I felt a shiver . . .
Dreams of a life to make with you, as only you can,
  You will always be to me my beautiful, most beautiful man . . .
Lucky am I, to have found such love,
  You and I, have been bound by God above . . .
Let the best be yet to come in our future,
  My family and yours will love us, that is sure . . .
For best wishes will be sent to us, for a beautiful start,
  Celebrate when we shall be together, and never again will part . . .

Send Me Your Soul

Send me your soul,
    And I'll send you mine . . .
Surrender your heart, to me,
    Yes, please do it, one more time . . .
For I shall keep it close,
    And watch it ever so near . . .
I will bless it each day,
    Perhaps with one pure tear . . .
If I can love you just once,
    Make it so perfect you'll see . . .
You shall dwell on it,
    The memory, for all eternity . . .
Yet, I can't just have one time with you,
    The pleasures you give,
I beg-give me more,
    It cannot be,
For I want it all,
    All of you,
From here at present,
    Until eternity . . .
I'll keep your soul safe,
    As you shall mine . . .
And our hearts shall be as one,
    For all, yes all of time . . .

Serenading Me Softly

Serenading me softly, with not music,
    But of soft words,
Enchanting my heart, distances apart,
Yet, the sound of the ocean gently rolling in,
    As the moonlight dances upon her,
Invokes me closer and I feel,
As do your words,
    Transform me to that place,
We magically go,
    To rest our feet upon,
    The softness of the sand,
The aura of my soul, lit up for you,
Empowering me to intricate you,
    Into my being,
As we stroll and seek,
    Our serenity within,
Enjoying the glow of this first born full moon,
    Since our celestial show,
And as that Sunday night did pass unto the next day,
Those beautiful words,
    I would always hear him say,
For it's his lips do hear,
    Whispering to me,
    The sweetest of sounds,
Magically taking me places,
Magically turning me around,
    As I awaken to find,
    The greatest of a new dawn . . .

She Knew

She knew-
    It was he,
    It was he . . .
That had turned her whole life around,
As she sat nestled in the quaintness, of Myrtle,
She knew-
    It was he,
    It was he . . .
That when she touched her heart to escape too,
Who captivated her heart,
She knew-
    It was he,
    It was he . . .
That when she gazed into the dark and saw-
The horizon and the sky,
She knew what he had said,
She knew-
    It was he,
    It was he . . .
That she wanted to share the moonlight with,
To gaze into his eyes only,
She knew-
    It was he,
    It was he . . .
That she wanted to walk,
As far as she could see, or possibly wonder,
She knew-
    It was he,
    It was he . . .

That when they sat on that bench,
She would remember, that kiss good-by,
That perfect farewell, For-
She knew-
    It was he,
    It was he . . .
When she sat here gazing at the sea,
It would totally capture herself,
And it was he that made her a woman,
And she made him her man . . . And-
She knew-
    It was he,
    It was he . . .
No matter what she did, or where she went,
If he was not there, Always-And,
She knew-
    It was he,
    It was he . . .
When she closed her eyes at night,
And heard her heart, they both would come back,
To the sea, together, and love would blossom,
Totally, because-
She knew-
    It was he,
    It was he . . .

She Looked at The Face

She looked at the face, so perfect in her mind,
    As he came closer, oh he is so kind, so kind . . .
Roses for her, always did he bring,
    With passion only for him, her voice, shall soon sing . . .
Oh the blessings from above, she has her boy,
    Leaning ever so closer, he too, has his toy . . .
A gentleman he shall, one day become,
    For he waits for his lass, not as some . . .
He just takes a look, and he knows deep within,
    How possibly could he ever be without her, his lady, his Lynn . . .

She Stood as a Babe

She stood as a babe, perhaps one, perhaps two,
Gazing so simplistically what could she do . . .
Hanging tightly, her doll in her hand,
Never knowing years later, her life would be grand . . .
And she met a man, gave it up with a wink,
She knew in her heart, she didn't need to think . . .
He was the one, who was with her from the start,
He was the soul deep in her heart . . .
Innocence as a babe can not return,
Yet, from the start, she knew, never having to learn,
It was her heart, That would burn . . .

Slipping Into a Trance of Delight

My sweetheart, blasting through me,
    With a sense of warmth,
Shaking my body into a constant, rhythm of-
    Sensuous sensations over and over,
Stopping to catch my breath, for an instant,
    Until it begins again,
Slipping into a trance of delight,
Awakening to an escapade of more delight,
Channeling your love into a constant,
Rhythm-sensation of love . . .
Where does it begin? Where does it end?
Wandering aimlessly deeper into channels of-
Wild discovery, realizing their strength,
Thrusting my inner core,
    Totally acknowledging you,
Relaxing-I absorb totally all of it,
    Not knowing if I could ever experience,
    This pleasure again,
I ask, not why-I accept, Enjoy!
Salivating for more-I engulf all of it,
Understanding, appreciating and thanking God,
For the most precious gift he could ever give me,
    Feelings for you, feelings full,
And love so profound it takes me away,
Releasing me from responsibilities here,
Except to enjoy and fully love my sweetest,
My darling, my sweetheart,
Today, tomorrow and as long as I am,
Grateful to have him in my loving arms to stay . . .

So, He Smiled

So, He smiled when he thought of her face,
　　That little bit of heaven, his ace . . .
She was the one, that turned his life around,
　　He knew in his heart, where he was bound . . .
Where they could fly, as free as the wind, be,
　　All cares aside, they both would glee . . .
He asked the Lord, how long shall he wait,
　　All good things take patience, even your fate . . .
My love shall be mine, one sweet day,
　　She will lay beside you, you shall have your way . . .
All longing shall vanish, when she belongs to you,
　　Never be parted, forget the night you were blue . . .
Just remember that smile, that caught your eye,
　　Never again, shall you tell her good-by . . .

So Sweet When I First See Your Face

So sweet when I first see your face,
   Knowing our feelings so strong, they could never be erased . . .
My heart thumps when you first come close,
   Kissing and hugging you give me my first dose . . .
I want to reach out, and draw you in,
   Feelings tempting me, where do I begin . . .
A pleasant hello, I contain myself, at first,
   My heart racing rapidly, it wants to burst . . .
Forgetting all reasoning we begin to kiss,
   Such passion ignites—I can feel pure bliss . . .
Then touching begins at first just one hand,
   I cuddle a little closer—I touch his band . . .
He whispers sweet thoughts to me in my ear,
   Dare I feel more—yes I want to hear . . .
Let the suit cases linger, I have such a thought,
   We'd better hurry upstairs, before we get caught . . .
Don't dance with me darling, I need you right away,
   Come to me quickly, I love you—let us lay . . .
It just feels so perfect, to melt in his arms,
   All negativity erased, just peace, no harms . . .
Then we wonder how we began again so fast,
   This passion never dies down-it just will last . . .
But next time around, we'll try to go slow,
   This will happen again, I guess we both really know . . .

Speak To Me

Speak to me with words not silence,
Silence hurts deeper, than my soul can handle,
Touch me-still softly with words,
Even harsh if they must be,
But, speak to me,
Allow silence not to enter therein,
What thoughts you carry-
When my mind does not hear,
Deep hurt does surround,
Even those so near,
Silence be not your friend,
Make it thy enemy,
What good comes from that,
Separations from love,
Anger and hatred soon to impose,
Rather yet, speak,
Let kind words reach out,
Love, So precious it can heal-
The harshest of cold,
For silence is death,
Allowing none to penetrate,
Let me in with your words-not silence,
And I to your mind will penetrate . . .

Surrender Your Soul

Surrender your soul to the warm ocean breeze, my dear,
    Let your being absorb natures beautiful sunset, so near . . .
As the seagulls do wander down the shore at dusk, sweet,
    Fill the moment; let your body have a rush, a treat . . .
See the beauty of each shell as they lay,
    Walking along the sand, sometimes the ocean touches,
    Begging you to stay . . .
And you do, absorbing each and every sound,
    Hearing the breeze whisper, magically she is around . . .
You are drawn back and back to this world, dear,
    The energy born from it unfurls, you hear . . .
Joining yourself to the oneness of creation, so grand,
    Knowing all the things their purpose to understand . . .
But the ocean it calls, and the love it sends out,
    Brings forth your destiny, making it clearer you shout . . .
I have found my truth, my hope, my dream,
    For he is with me, in my heart, and I scream . . .
Come enjoy this world its colors of orange and rust,
    Loving your woman here, caressing her bust . . .
Make passionate love, to hear her whisper I love you so true,
    While climaxing together under the sky so blue . . .
And ever so gently, stroking her softly just lay,
    Remember, she loves you so dearly, always she will stay . . .

Take Away All My Pain

Take away all my pain,
    Magically was everything aside,
Hold me close let me blend into you,
    As if all previous time-I have known,
Vanished, and time begins again,
    Let me touch just you,
    To feel sensations of love,
Wished for, yet not known,
The powers, vanishing all hurt buried so deep,
Releasing it, into an openness, for it to leave-
And leave me, Refreshed, Rejuvenated, Anew,
Hold me-while I feel security filtering in,
Embracing all parts of my being,
Peace arrived,
You have found a way-
To love, me for me,
Not what I can accomplish, or be,
Yet only me-myself,
Not understanding-why,
Feeling needs to hold back,

Yet wanting this man to know,
    Trust-I Do,
    Love-I Have,
Yet, pulling and tugging deep secret thoughts,
Trust—I want to,
    My thoughts are scared,
Scared to not be able to have the strength to cope,
Yet-I Do,
    I Trust,
    I Love,
His arms held tight,
    Will allow me to release, release, release . . .
Until a peace, comes,
And I know peace . . .
For the Lord gave me you,
As my peace,
My dove, my beautiful, beautiful, so beautiful,
    Pure Dove, My Love . . .

Take Me Away To Places I've Never Been

Take me away to places I've never been,
Deep within my mortal soul, we both do wander,
Feelings we sought from our distant past,
Surrendering my heart, I respond, my love, it is you at last.

Take me away to places I've never been,
Gathering feelings toward you, with welcoming thoughts,
Dreaming of long ago ages, I start to recall too much,
Wondering how this—my completeness, love, it is you at last.

Take me away to places I've never been,
Wisk me there, and from your loins shall I follow,
My soul you have taken, with love so profound,
Experiencing desires, concealed, love, unravel at last.

Take me away to places I've never been,
Where feelings hold truth, and all shall be known,
My days shall turn to dusk, and dare I shall hope,
Paradise doth appear, alas to experience it with you . . .

Take Me Away Where You And I Alone Exist

Take me away-
Where you and I alone exist,
Fantasies come to life,
And you alone are mine,
To satisfy and defend all odds,
We've mastered the art of seduction,
The oneness of togetherness,
Our yearnings have melted deep-
Into each other,
Blended into one whirl of bliss-
That bathes us with truth,
Unfolding for each other to-
Experience and rejuvenate,
So to enrich us daily,
As we pass each hour,
Waiting for the other,
Joyfully until my Sweetheart,
Captivates me,
And whisks me away-
Yet, for another . . .

Take Me To a Place

Take me to a place, secure in your arms,
Where I can float away, away-
Safe in that place, so near to your heart,
Talk to me softly; help me wash away my fears,
Let all insecurities melt away, away-
Let them not pass, my portals of love,
You only shall enter, my dear, my dear,
Whispering magically, just let go, let go,
Let love encircle and intwine, intwine-
Help me to free my mind,
From memories past, sometimes hurt washes in,
Save me with your purest of love, so dear, so near,
Let me feel, as we savor,
Loves tempting surprise, as you whisper so close,
Let go, let go, as you slowly move inward,
Clinging I whisk away,
Spoil not, by thoughts from past, try not,
To enter our magical cocoon,
Yet, patience still-give, oh loveliest of men,
Your angel asks this only of you . . .

Take My Hands

Take my hands, and speak to them,
For I am as you, a child of this universe,
An old soul perhaps, with wisdom to share,
I chose but to follow another path . . .

Take my hands, and look into my heart,
For it is there for you to see,
God's total wisdom,
And divine light and love surrounding me . . .

Take my hands, and look into my eyes as you speak,
They bring you messages, beyond my words,
I am enlightened with gifts that My Creator has given,
For you to just reach out and take,

Take my hands, I feel as you,
Listen to them as they say,
God created them a little more perfect,
So they as our Father, can speak to you . . .

This was written for Steve, who speaks as
beautiful with his hands as his eyes . . .

Tenderly Calling Me

Tenderly calling you-
　　Captivating your curiosity,
　　As you have before-
　　Since centuries past,
Opened my bedroom door,
Aroused my un-swept sensations inside-
　　To awaken,
　　Feel the demands, set forth by your essence,
So deep, do I feel, you dwell inside-
　　Every inch of my awareness,
Welcomes you, to venture, to exist,
　　Exhilarating me into your being,
　　As you have forever done,
We are encircled together as one,
　　My mind, my spirit, my body-
　　Encased securely into your being,
Safe-I release everything, I have,
　　Everything, I want to have,
　　All, with you,
Totally-to complete you,
　　Satisfy, release all hurt that ever was,
　　All pain now gone,
　　All emotions set still,

For I have found you so perfect,
Unexplainable, perhaps,
　　To maybe a few,
Yet, to those who understand,
　　It is just-
　　It is true-
I have always known this feeling,
　　You bring it toward the surface,
Hidden, until we meet again,
To surrender, I had to,
　　So perfect you were,
My knight who had come back,
　　To bring forth his lady,
　　From the darkness, into the light,
　　And glow they would,
As our Lord intended them too,
For love will find a way back,
　　To its center, Its Soul-
　　To become whole, as I complete you,
　　You do me,
Love encircling us, in this bliss-for eternity . . .

That Kiss

That kiss . . .
You know the one that you dream of,
  And suddenly it's there,
    You know the one you've always imagined,
    Could make you float on air . . .
You know the one that passion ignites from,
  You know the one you can't let go of,
    Until you come . . .
You know the one that ignites every flame inside,
  You know the one, you had after your long
  Midnight ride . . .
You know the one that pulls you to soar, Baby
  Do you want to the roar . . .
You know the one-it is That Kiss . . .
  You know it is, your beautiful Miss . . .

The Beauty Of Your Soul

The beauty of your soul mesmerizes me,
    Into a quiet tranquility of calm,
As I sit contemplating the future,
    I am at peace,
    For I have known,
    The utmost love, that God to grant, has given us,
Surreal, sometimes,
    Yet, I accept it,
    For what it is,
Giving, understanding, quiet, kind,
    It is mine,
    To be shared with him,
For I love to give him, all that I have,
    Not wanting, in return,
To give, just because, I love too,
    To feel his joy, his grace,
And to remember, that beauty, that face,
    When we make love,
    That mesmerizes me,
    Into such a calm . . .

The First Flower

The first flower you gave me, was a perfect rose,
    I kept it a month, smelling it nightly with my nose . . .
The flowers this year, give me still so much delight,
    Saying to them nightly, a heartfelt goodnight . . .
Your kindness I appreciate so much, I just melt,
    My darling, this afternoon it's you I felt . . .
Love, what a heartfelt goodnight your love gave me,
    Filling me up, only between us, to a tee . . .
Darling the words you whisper send me a swirl,
    Countless blessings the Lord sent me; I'm your girl . . .
Telling me forever and one day, we shall never part,
    Holding you only in the center of my heart . . .
And tonight, when finally after my work be done,
    I'll cuddle up next to you, my love, for a night of fun . . .

The Lord Gave You To Me

The Lord gave you to me, and who am I to question,
You have touched my spirit deeply, as you already know,
My love, my perception of being, is clouded over, with and entire glow,
Shining so bright and clear, as none has done before,
Yet, my love he doth protest, the love he has been given,
Accept my darling accept, be glad, understand,
For blessings must not be questioned,
Contentment will surround you,
And reassurance will be given,
This love I've not experienced before, I woman for a man,
The vastness of my knowledge is quenched, with just one thought,
Excitement intercedes us, while joy of you over bounds,
Never finish with me, my darling, for I could not ever exist,
Your essence always caresses me, surely always think of this,
You ravish my inner being,
Expounding happiness of such magnitude,
It enriches my inner sanctity of self,
Knowing one truth, my sweetheart,
Is acknowledging the acceptance of just,
Yes being content with loving,
No other, my love, but you . . .

The Magical Wonder of Real Love

The magical wonder of real love,
    Can touch your soul and transport you,
    Endlessly into streams and beams of pleasure,
Carrying you, endlessly through the night,
    With the passion you always dreamed of,
    But never felt before,
Until, he came, he patiently waited,
    For you to decide, his fate, his destiny, his truth,
Another beautiful night of seduction,
Yet, so intense, intoxicating-
    The pulsations of love,
    Danced throughout my being,
My sweetheart, had taken me through,
    The night until the dawn,
    When I awakened,
And I looked up into the heavens,
    And thanked my Creator,
    For what he had given me,
For, few shall know,
    The wonderment of love,
For his soul, has melted into mine,
And the creator, in bringing us together,
    Has truly been so divine,
We are together,
    As our hopes-desire us to be,
Perfectly achieving,
My femininity in his manliness,
    Let me stay,
And ponder, forever,
    My love in his as such,
This is how-I shall live . . .

The Silence That We Hear

Though we speak, two different ways,
    I can feel your inner thoughts,
Your eyes convey, the deepness of your soul,
    Communication is felt at an inner level,
    Words need not unfold,
Let hands manifest, the beauty of those words,
    As only you can tell,
And those of us, who reach beyond,
    Can truly hear your words,
    The silence that we hear—

Dedicated to my all of my Deaf friends, I love you all

The Sweetest Treasure

The sweetest treasure, I was ever allowed to unwrap,
    So beautiful when I hold your head, upon my lap . . .
Ever so close and content may you be,
    Stroking your arm softly, you begin to glee . . .
My love, always it is of you, I ponder,
    Closely you lay, beside me, as my head does wander . . .
You are a stranger, to me no more,
    Together, our love, shared, it will pour . . .
Surround by majestic grace so full,
    Your arms embraced me, with a pull . . .
And the sweetest of a kiss, did land on one lip,
    So sensuous feelings as in a dance dip . . .
Continuing to embrace those kisses so fine,
    My angelic love knew, I could never un-wine . . .
He would captivate my heart,
    Whether kissing or at rest, he had to be himself-the best . . .
So lay your head softly on my lap,
    Together, content, satisfied we shall nap . . .
And hold the man, I love so close to me,
    Endearing messages of love, between us, as it should . . .

The Sweetness Of Your Scent

The sweetness of your scent,
    Amazes me-as no other . . .
Gliding me inward to embrace,
    Every moment I'm allowed,
And he lay so content next to her,
    She engulfed his whole as he slept,
Touching so gently his loins,
    Pondering if he knew, she was near,
Or had sleep embraced him so,
    His gentleness was at rest,
Turning so slow, allowing touches to yet sustain,
    A fire that ceases to decline,
She too slept, whisked away-
    To a beautiful place, they both would share,
Content, life was dusk to near dawn,
    Sleep would conquer, where two lovers lay,
And she'll wait for yet one more day to shine,
    Until they tell each other a beautiful line . . .

The Man I Adore

The man I adore,
　　So soft your voice when it whispered to me,
Those words I love to hear,
Wake me-my love-awake me,
To precious words-that comfort my soul,
　　So beautiful, to hear,
　　As my tears of joy appear,
For I know you long for me,
　　As I do you,
And we surrender our hearts to join,
　　As we drifted so far, this morn,
Unaware, could I return,
　　I must,
　　But love, oh, that love so strong,
So passionate, did fully consume,
　　All of me, until the dawn appeared,
And we both whispered our soft bye byes . . .

The Time We Spent Together

The time we spent together, with each other will always last,
  Although we enjoyed so much pleasure, time still goes too fast . . .
Treasures of you will I carry, in my heart to always remember,
  Sweetheart, my whole, my soul, my being-to you, I did surrender . . .
With such passion to glide us from day until night,
  You gave me completeness, by showing me the true light . . .
With all of this love, knowledge, and memories shall I keep,
  Allowing me to go back to you anytime, never allowing you to weep . . .
For true love has strengthen me, everyday that I will now live,
  Melted in my heart, completeness, that is what you-did give . . .

The Way To My Soul

The way to my soul-You already know,
You are there,
I can feel,
With closed eyes your presence surrounds me,
Pulsations of you and I-beating as one,
Knowing, understanding my thoughts-You do,
Emotions cascading my every concern-my care,
You who know my soul,
The way to its inner core,
You live it, beside of me,
Or distances-we dare not go,
For you alone, fill my desires,
Never masquerading your truth,
For you feel those pulsations, the same as I-
As I do yours-
Your connections come, to my true sense of happiness,
I know as only you do,
That, it is real,
So real, your soul wants to hide,
Not unveiling itself at this time,
Analyzing moment after moment,
Until you explode, into questioning, why?
Run my soul-escape, these emotions so wise,
As though so strong, how can I dare survive,
You breathe-only to escape the sweat,
That inevitably appears upon your brow,
Slow cautious bits of air,
Meditating, realizing, there is no escape,
And love will ultimately win . . .

The Waves Came Crashing In

The waves came crashing in,
 Forcefully as the portal opened,
 Without hesitation,
Longing for the gush, so magnificent,
 It would fill her every breath,
 As if dancing around,
 The rhythm of the moment,
 Soothed her, mesmerizing her thoughts,
 Like nothing before,
The waves crushed and beat against,
 Her once calm shores,
Assuring her that life was rich,
 With satisfaction just waiting,
 For the light house to give the signal,
The perfect seduction of the wave,
 Flowing freely into the channel,
Allowed it to find its purpose,
 It's reason for being,
As the wave settled, it knew it had reached,
 Every corner, every aspect,
 Could be felt,
It was complete,
The cycle had reached its orgasm,
 And perfection,
 That the wave they had sought,
 Was fulfilled in that port,
Again it would churn,
 And again, she would open her gates,
 To welcome the roar, the thundering of passion,
For this truly was her life,
And the ocean her home . . .

Thinking of You

Thinking of you . . .
Contemplating no other,
Life's mysteries at work,
I function, I breathe, I walk,
Yet, deep
Deeply you sit,
Inside my soul,
Accompanying me, everywhere,
Everyone I talk too,
My thought goes back, to you,
I hope you are happy,
As you can be,
Silent, we can not speak,
Dependent on yet, our heart,
We are connected that way,
Thinking of you,
Always,
As the rain rustles downward,
Touching all we know,
Dancing upon me, as I walk,
Everything is you,
Every thought, I wish to tell you,
To hear your voice,
Yes darling,
Thinking of you,
Always, Darling, Always . . .

To See The Absolute Beauty Of This World

To see the absolute beauty of this world,
As suddenly spin into my existence,
Enchanting music whispers to me all day,
Dancing cascades me, yet allowing me to play,
Life has renewed itself into a new meaning,
Signs and miracles draw near, toward God I am leaning,
Love has been surpassed, by knowledge from above,
Bring forth such devotion, a new meaning for a dove,
For this love can not be measured in a simple way,
It is so powerful, it truly is meant to stay,
I love this angel with all of my heart,
I knew I loved my angel from the start,
I must realize, this I must face,
I can sum up his existence—he is full of Grace . . .

To Understand The True Meaning Of Love

To understand the true meaning of love . . .
    Is to be tested . . .
    A test that may seem too impossible to pass,
    A test that may be questioned,
    Why was I given this to bare?
Yet, through the testing of love,
    We find sure truth, wholeness, blessedness, and joy . . .
    That we question no further,
Yet, chose to accept,
    For love is one of the greatest gifts to be given . . .
    And testing is a gift in faithfulness to our Lord . . .

Total Completeness Inner Bursting Of Joy

Full of ecstasy of this moment must be captured,
You whisper for my knowledge, this may be our last,
This magnitude of love so unreal, must
Somehow be absorbed in me,
And put in a place to remember . . .
Surrounding my inner most soul,
Circles of beautiful light abound,
Pulsating our souls together, as they intermix,
Hearts being as one, never missing a beat . . .
Total completeness, inner bursting of joy,
From avenues of desires captured, radiating outwards . . .
Till the whiteness of lights, purest of thoughts,
And knowledge of knowing,
The true meaning of the word, love . . .
Holding these moments as our truth,
Fully aware, yet unwilling to accept,
Once could it, be enough,
Wanting, craving, the physical expressiveness,
Yet, satisfied and contempt,
In the acceptance of one absolute perfect,
Point of being, and it was with You . . .

Touching So Soft

And he lay there, touching so soft her leg,
Ever so gently, to start moving every emotion inside her,
He knew, nothing had to be done,
Just a stroke, as simple as a touch,
His toe, his foot, somehow something just touched,
And she was his, never resistant,
To the feel of his senses,
Drawing her closer, where gentleness would come,
And if he dared move,
Yes move upon her now,
Explosions would burst-feelings would fly,
And the quiet that might have been,
Would have awakened,
Into chills of sheer delight, beautiful passion,
That had yet started, with one soft touch,
Of that perfect leg-hers,
Yes, hers alone . . .

Treasure You, I Do

Treasure you, I do,
Every morning, as I look down upon you,
Memorizing each piece of your precious being,
Engulfing these moments of oneness, closeness,
That we have shared,
Capturing it, as if a time capsule could be made,
And opened when needed,
To envelope my soul, into pure bliss,
Yes, I look, early before dawn,
Before life has a way, of change,
When I can still feel,
His breathe upon my sheet,
His feet touching, yet oh so soft,
And his whisper, knowing I am awake,
Treasure you, I do,
For each moment is a gift,
Of love, with such meaning and care,
To have witnessed this joy,
To have partaken of your majesty,
Has given me enough,
To fill pages upon pages,
Of endless devotions, syllables of meaning,
Of treasures you have given to me,
To fill my grateful heart . . .

Unbreakable

I thought we were unbreakable you and I,
Life has a way of changing things,
Unimaginable circumstances colliding into karmas repaid,
Debts to settle, emotions running wild-
Why, is it us, I question,
Who ponders that circumstance,
Beyond what we promised,
Beyond what we ever knew possible,
I wait, quietly,
Yet restless nights,
I feel,
You, holding me,
Tantalizing me into yet another thought,
Of why, I cannot quiet this heart, any more,
I can not-stop,
This one serene existence,
I have no power,
He holds my emotions,
As if a little piece of me,
Needs to be strung back on a pearl-based necklace,
They have gravitated into space,
And you hold the key,
The twine to put them together,
The essence of our truth,
Lies in-but-you,
Rise up-hear your thoughts,
Speak to me, your mind, allow yourself,
Your heart-to be free . . .

Unexpected, Unplanned

Unexpected, unplanned you gently came,
    One sweet December morning,
      My man claimed his dame,
As she always knew,
    He was the one who had her heart,
He came to her rescue,
    And excitement all burst apart,
Sparks flew, as fireworks appeared,
    July 4th had arrived,
      On this quiet December day,
His passion burned so deep,
    His damsel dared not move,
Love was all around her,
    And filled her every groove,
The wildness rustled in,
    And filtered every space,
Once more, darling, have I fallen from grace,
Yet, he was the man,
The man of her dreams, she knew-
That every passion, she ever had-
    Had-suddenly came true,
She longed for one,
    One more time with him,
And yes,
Her darling-
He-did again, Begin,
This love was pure,
    Satisfying and true,
And her Sweetheart,
    Would start again, Anew!!!

Unthinkable Joy Has Burst Unto Me

Unthinkable joy has burst unto me,
Awakening me with such pleasure,
Unbeknoweth, but to you and me,
Pulsating deep within places never explored,
Envelopes of swirls connecting senses beyond my imagination,
And escaping me to places with passions I've lived before,
Minds not being able to phantom such deep thoughts,
I ponder how does this wonderment come to me,
How deep can my sensations reach?
At last I know, it is not this world that can handle such joy-
The thrill it escapes this reality scheme,
And wanders me into an element unknown,
Yet willing to explore-I escape,
My Sweetheart and me,
Escape to a safe haven, where love has been conquered,
And knowledge of it opened up for us to enjoy,
As such we cannot imagine,
Love has to be earned,
We look, seek, hope, and savor what we are allowed-
For this love to powerful for words-
Must be accepted as it is-
A gift from above,
So precious, so few-
It has been given to me and you . . .

We Are as One with The Universe

We are as one with the universe,
    Both you and I,
A passion reborn,
    A full sense of being,
Completely known,
For we have traversed these worlds,
    From near and far,
Both ages past, and now,
Before in that distant land-
Parted-a love unfilled,
Un-leased into the depths of . . .
    Our souls to replenish,
And they will at that,
    Now secure, Knowing-
Pass not again from me,
For I dare not wait,
    Centuries upon centuries,
Lifetimes living, without your touch,
Passion like this, needs to ignite,
To burn until the flame cannot be seen,
Feelings hid down, ages have passed,
Until reuniting with such a look,
Eyes comforted with a reunited soul,
Held back by tears release . . .

We Might Never Get Another

We might not get another, as you begin to say,
That meaning hurting so deep, I began to pray,
Knowing that truth, alas I must face someday,
Devouring thoughts of which, I cannot be certain . . .

We might never get another, as you began to say,
Grudging inward deep thoughts, sweetly remembering,
This magnitude of such love, so surreal I shall recall,
Pulsating of our souls, as love doth forth intertwine . . .

We might never get another, as you began to say,
So sweet this completeness will touch me, for yet another day,
Days they turn to weeks, as months they shall too disappear,
Time for us will be eternity, do not fear, my sweet . . .

We might never get another, as you began to say,
Physical expressions, alas be yet so true,
Contemplating acceptance of this time, spent only with you,
Freely aware, my love, alas there will not be another . . .

Whisper Sweet Nothings to Me

Whisper sweet nothings to me, while I sleep,
Carry me off quickly-intensify me so deep . . .
Just as this morn, satisfy my whim,
Make love from dawn, until the lights go dim . . .
Whirling through my psyche, never letting go,
Moments turn to hours, never ceasing to glow . . .
And the magic continues, between you and I,
Sometimes taking one more breathe, before I sigh . . .
Take me on your journey, swirl me inside of you,
Cascade your thoughts in front of me, before I do . . .
For your precious power, has stolen my heart away,
Never to be the same, my love is here to stay . . .
Come quickly back this evening, I dare not be alone,
Fill my body completely, before you phone . . .
Never allow us not to remember, the feelings, oh so rare,
Fill my whole soul with your essence-make me feel . . .

With Such Tenderness

With such tenderness coming over me,
Pushing me deeper and deeper into delight,
Ignoring outward forces-I remained-
For you to carry me into morning light,
For love I had seen with this man before,
But more-yet-I craved more,
As none I had before,
So powerful, do true-
Our love was surely bestowed,
I told him secrets, as I lay close,
Told him how I felt,
Of his soft yet strong hand,
For I do feel, I celebrated today,
For a ray of sunshine awakened my day,
And the force of love, so strong,
It did give to me, so clear,
My Sweetheart is with me,
So very near,
I love him, Lord deeper,
Let him always know,
He is mine forever,
And in my heart,
He doth Glow . . .

Words are a Powerful Thing

Words are a powerful thing,
A gift given to us,
To express our thoughts,
And teach us,
Use them with respect,
For through them,
Come the wisdom,
Of all the ages,
Which is Knowledge . . .

Originally published in The International Library
of Poetry-Enlightened Shadows, 2001

You Always Knew My Inner Thought

You always knew my inner thought,
Our hopes, our dreams, it was you my love, I sought . . .
I waited for you secretly through the years,
Always knowing you would arrive to erase all my tears . . .
Strong I built myself-the best that I could,
Always longing for my true love, alas I should . . .
Your gift to me was an inner peace,
My gift to you-my heart I was to release . . .
My happiness from you has come-it so fast,
My sweetheart you have appeared at last . . .
For the pain from our separation-was so long,
Our love that bound us together is ever so strong . . .
To give it totally to the man of my dreams,
He alas gave me everything, oh my heart, it gleams . . .
Hold me and keep my heartache at bay,
And I will caress you my love, through far away . . .
For I've longed for you to come and be mine,
Fill my senses-delightfully-so fine . . .
You are my angel, my gift from the Lord,
We have come forth together, on our own accord . . .
Please never go now from me, stay forever mine,
We have come together, we are complete and totally fine . . .

You Appeared

You appeared as bright as a ray of sunshine,
    You appeared my man who makes every problem, I have fine . . .
You appeared my knight in shining armor,
    You appeared blessing me with knowledge to my central core . . .
You appeared a smile I could never resist,
    You appeared your words explaining what's on my list . . .
You appeared cause you teach me what I need to yet learn,
    You appeared and one whisper, I remember, for you, I yearn . . .
You appeared as magic a gift from our Lord above,
    You appeared to always give me-your everything, your Love . . .

You Are My Soul

Caress in the moonlight,
    Thoughts of you, to my delight . . .
So grand I remember,
    Way back the month after September . . .
When your arms engulfed me,
    As the moon and stars we would see . . .
And whisper did you,
    Of love so beautiful and true . . .
That I await, or next week, fate,
    Love shall surround myself, my mate . . .
Blossoming inward until it will burst,
    Causing nothing but wishing you first . . .
And moonlit strolls shall enhance the feel,
    Causing sensuous feelings, oh so real . . .
Trying to control all the emotion I have,
    Enjoying moments with you, my fav . . .
Holding you gently, memorizing the night,
    Never letting go, till the dawn, it will light . . .
But memories we shall make, for a lifetime to last,
    Our time together, runs to fast . . .
I love you now more than ever before,
    You my darling, feel my whole core . . .

You Ask Me

You ask me to touch my heart,
I do,
Waiting no more, tasks done,
I come to you-desires unwind,
You touch, you feel, you love,
Then as magically, as two are one,
Your force plunges inside me,
We are one,
In one country, not two,
Together, as we should be,
All night, touching,
Cheek to cheek,
What else, could I ever desire,
Ever need,
I am thankful,
To have those arms,
They surround me,
That heart that fills mine,
That sense,
Of knowing he is there,
Complete in me,
Until I wake,
And carry on,
Tasks, they need to be done,
Until my Love,
Is back inside me . . .

You Call

You call-
    Suddenly everything is fine . . .
You touch-
    Suddenly you are mine . . .
You breathe-
    Suddenly life is worth living . . .
You sigh-
    Suddenly the world seems forgiving . . .
You kiss-
    Suddenly I turn and blush . . .
You caress-
    Suddenly, oh what a rush . . .
You care-
    Suddenly the world is fine . . .
You love-
    Suddenly I know you are mine . . .

You Came To Me

You came to me, when I needed you, with love . . .
It fills me time after time, so sweetly . . .
Embodying me, excitement rushes in . . .
Savoring the deep penetrations I feel . . .
Releasing your essence, I feel so secure . . .
Glowing warmth awaits you, advancing alas . . .
Passions escalate, joining one to each other . . .
Venturing outwards, fulfillment is done . . .
Craving yet more, always of you . . .
Until you fill me once more, sweetheart . . .
It will only be you, alas-only be you . . .

You freed My Soul

You freed my soul-
From pain beyond imagination . . .
Depths unexplainable,
For grief knows-
How to live in a heart,
With manly ways, and a gentle touch-
You freed me, as no other,
My soul gave thanks to yours,
Blessings bestowed upon you always,
Connections realized,
As though our lifetime had not been apart,
Dimensions crossed-
Where only your lovers heart be found,
Passions exploding, unraveling experiences-
Yet, to be transversed,
And we wait, patiently, silently,
You who freed this soul of mine,
Allow not troubles to bear upon your heart,
Instead cherish deeply-
The soul you thus freed . . .

You Have Filled Me

You have filled me up to completion,
Where I could never want for more,
All desires, all wants have been exceeded,
Tempestuous thoughts have been filled,
    As the rush of you swept through my body,
    As it danced into dimensions yet unknown,
You wove your wonderment past my heart,
    To every inch of every vibration,
    That has been set,
My breath still is not down,
    It hangs on a place-my mind still is,
I can't reach reality-it is no more,
I have escaped,
I am at such peace,
    It is nirvana-
    Far better than drugs used by some,
More perfect, those expectations,
    I could have dreamed,
Just your thoughts,
    Unleases-vibrant mysteries of lust,
    Compounding into a thrust,
    My heart accepts,
It wants more, but it is content,
    Because all of you came,
    All of you given,
And all of you I have known-
Just as I to you,
Are exactly the-Same . . .

You Know When You Are With Her

You know when you are with her-you fly,
  Excelling all expectations, romancing,
  Letting the world go by . . .
You melt so deep-your worries fly away,
  Only goodness and beautiful thoughts,
  Now, will stay . . .
Unstoppable, yes all the world, is your stage,
  Together, always until a very old age . . .
Is she worth it, they all will ask,
  Remembering life times with her,
  She wears no mask . . .
Just love surrounds her, and this she gave you,
  Together, we're unstoppable,
  Perfect and true . . .

You Reach Out

You reach out,
    And touch the only hand,
    That can sooth your soul,
You reach out,
    And touch the only one,
    That releases your passions,
    Making you unfold,
You reach out,
    And know her heart,
    Is the half of yours-that fits,
You reach out,
    And capture all the comfort,
    All the hope, that ever was,
You reach out,
    And feel the deepness,
    As you reach the inner part of her,
You reach out,
    And suddenly, with one touch,
    Everything that was,
    And everything that will be,
    Is at peace, Because you-
    Touched her . . .

You Remember

You remember . . .
>That tickle that you give,
>The first time you touch, again-

You remember . . .
>The scent that lingers over her,
>Stirring you magically deeper, beside her-

You remember . . .
>The simplicity of just wanting,
>To be together-

You remember . . .
>The sigh cascading from her lips,
>Showing her anticipation, before you kiss-

You remember . . .
>It is she-somehow that transforms you back,
>To your innocent youth-

You remember . . .
>Just that snuggle, when rain appears at the pane,
>And her glance, everything is suddenly fine-

Yes,
You remember . . .
>You did grow up, but memorized that face, hers-

You remember . . .
>It was she, that you sought,
>She, you looked for, from your youth-

You remember . . .
>And just lay back and giggle,
>For she is yours, as her laugh, so fine . . .

You Sleep

You sleep,
    Peace surrounds you,
    In your knowing-she is near,
So you sleep,
    To awaken to those precious words you wait to hear . . .
Darling, come
    I have made you a surprise,
    Anticipating, what delight,
    Shall come over your palate,
    What other fantasies are in her mind,
Hesitating, not,
    You dare not too,
Her magic draws you,
    Closer to her, your beloved,
But now, you are still asleep,
    Asleep, as peaceful as though-
    Still a child,
Knowing not,
    This fierce reality of a world we lie upon,
Not knowing anger, revenge, or words of hate,
Just love, pure love,
Given to you first by the Lord,
    And now she gives it to you,
    Such love, such grace, such joy,

And so you sleep,
Unaware, of troubles,
    Just peace, a peace surrounded and secure,
    Because, she is near,
And she was given to you,
    All you longed for, and more,
    As you did also,
So sleep, my angel, my love,
    Let not a single hurt,
    Inflict upon your soul, your being,
May you sleep and dance the night with me,
    In your dreams,
    As we sway our bodies together,
    In harmonic dance,
    Gliding our bodies inward,
    For there, they will slide,
Tantalizing us, rushing our hearts-breathless,
    In the most seductive of thoughts,
You and I forever will be one,
    Totally, pure and whole, always,
Just sleep,
    Sleep, my love, my one,
    And secret places we shall go,
And awaken you will, secure, in our being . . .

You Need to Be With Me as Only You Can

You need to be with me, as only you can,
It bonds us forever, hand in hand,
Our hearts are together, as the spacious sky is blue,
Two hearts melted into one, our love so true . . .

You need to be with me, as only you can,
Deep down I need you, my beautiful man,
It is truth that drives desires inside so strong,
Our sensuous bodies colliding, what could be wrong . . .

You need to be with me, as only you can,
Don't take it lightly, go ahead seduce your woman,
We need to keep the fire, let love flow,
Stay with me tonight, fireworks will glow . . .

You need to be with me, as only you can,
Fantasize me off to wonderland and catch me if you can,
Shower me with stars and a moonlit night,
Caressing me oh so gently and holding me ever so tight . . .

You need to be with me, as only you can,
Our love will grow stronger, touching my sweet man,
You are my special Sweetheart, come to me let's play,
Kissing me, hugging me, and caressing me all day . . .

Your Beautiful, Beautiful Soul

Your beautiful, beautiful soul-
    Oh, I adore the essence of it,
    So true, filled with wisdom of truth,
    Sharing unselfishly with me . . .

Your beautiful, beautiful soul-
    Mine, yet for the world to experience,
    Outwardly giving of yourself,
    So generous, yet, needing not, praise . . .

Your beautiful, beautiful soul-
    It warms me to a glow,
    Every time I am reminded of you,
    You're everything, I could have asked for . . .

Your beautiful, beautiful soul-
    Intertwined with mine, to set me free,
    To see this world, from a new perspective,
    My life, I've changed so quickly . . .

Your beautiful, beautiful soul-
    Has taught me to love God, more than I thought possible,
    My inward thoughts have become so clear,
    You have revealed my essence to me . . .

Your beautiful, beautiful soul-
    Enlightened my thoughts, and set them free,
    What I thought my truth was,
    I start to wonder . . .

Your beautiful, beautiful soul-
    May it last through eternity,
    To love your God and Creator,
    And grow in peace and harmony . . .

Your Kiss, So Passionate, So True

Your kiss-
    So passionate, so true-
Yet, I wait another,
How can such passion evolve,
    From your lips,
Your touch-
Gentle, yet soothing-
Washing away hurt, buried, forgotten,
Released into the universe,
Through your touch,
Your smile-
Embracing, inviting, and knowing you, alone-
Feed my inside,
    My deepest thoughts,
    My life,
Your life-
Given to me, to embrace and enjoy,
    With you,
Along the many splendors-
    That are yet to come . . .

Your Promises Made

Your promises made-not to be broken,
Words spoken-only the truth,
God hears all, and records it in Heaven,
Say not to be, unless it is from your heart,
Deep within-unveil that wall,
That seems not to be penetrated,
Reveal your thoughts, desires to me,
For I know-
    I already feel,
    The troubles that bind you,
Release—let go,
Pull me deep,
    Within those walls-
    That try, to hide me out,
Release-for love alone can heal,
And Truth will set-
    Your burdens free,
    So we may sail . . .

Your Spirit Came

Your spirit came,
    And came upon me,
I allowed it too,
    Transversing dimensions,
    Freely arriving,
Intensifying me, providing me with a comfort,
    Only you can,
It gravitates downward,
    Pulling inch after inch,
    Into its clutch,
I want you to release,
    All over, filling my being,
    With your sense, your love,
    Your commitment,
And you do,
    Allowing me to hold,
    To experience, and give back to you,
Everything we now hold real,
    Everything we now call Truth . . .

Your Sweetness Conquered Me

Your sweetness conquered me, with a mighty force,
Engulfing my soul, I knew I had found my equal,
My half, my divine-all that I could wish for,
Encompassed into one being, a perfect design,
Fitting into me, as it should,
Totally allowing me the reason to be,
The reason I am,
As the Lord is I am,
I found what it is that I am,
It is you, my other half,
My yin, my yang, my soul mate,
For it's you I see, when I wake in the morn,
It is your breath that captivates my every move,
It is you I fall to sleep, longing to dream of,
It is, it is you,
Still the Sweetness that conquered me,
And the sweetness that remains,
The mightiest of force that engulfs my soul,
Acknowledging to it, its equal is here,
Its half has returned to its home . . .

You're the One That

You-the one that sends my heart to spin,
    My life-still-till you told it to begin . . .
Destiny set our paths as one,
    The angels declared their work was done . . .
We had been reunited to start,
    The two of us would have one heart . . .
We could try to separate,
    Surreal pain, we would debate . . .
Drawing us closer for comfort, we would crave,
    This certainty-I know, I would take to my grave . . .
For my soul mate has awakened my spark,
    My life shall never, be again in the dark . . .
Fresh thoughts and energies we shall now bear,
    Transforming to new realms, shall we dare . . .
Faith, spirituality, and love shall collide,
    As we journey onwards, on this ride . . .
Mastering my course, my teacher by my side,
    Energizing my thoughts, I shall abide . . .
And all though, shall love be our lesson to learn,
    I shall advance my studies, a masters I shall earn . . .
With you as my teacher, my friend, my love,
    For it is He our Master, who has blessed us both from above . . .

You're The Reason Our Country is Strong

Every life it has a reason,
We do not question, but rely on Thee,
Some are chosen soldiers to protect us,
Others stay home as they were meant to be,
It is not up to us to know our mission,
Only to follow faithfully in Thee,
Thank-you soldiers for your service,
We respect and will be loyal to Thee,
For your sacrifices you endured,
For all your pain and misery,
We thank-you more than words can say,
Please be assured we feel this way . . .

Powerful Prayers that all of us can benefit from:

Powerful Prayer to The Holy Spirit

Holy Spirit, you who solve all problems, who light all roads, so that I can attain my goal. You who give me the Divine gift to forgive and to forget all evil against me and that in all instances of my life you are with me. I want this short prayer to thank you for all things and to confirm once again that I never want to be separated from you even in spite of all material illusions. I wish to be with you in eternal glory. Thank you for your Mercy toward me and mine.

The person must say this prayer for 3 consecutive days, after 3 days the favor will be granted even if it may appear difficult. This prayer must be published immediately after the favor is granted without mentioning the favor. Only your initials should appear at the bottom. SLB

St. Jude's Novena

May the Sacred Heart of Jesus be adored, glorified, loved and preserved throughout the world, now and forever.

Sacred Heart of Jesus, pray for us. St. Jude, worker of miracles, pray for us.

Say this prayer 9 times a day and by the eighth day your prayer will be answered. It has never been known to fail. Thank you St. Jude. SLB

Prayer to The Virgin Mary

"O Most Beautiful Flower of Mount Carmel, fruitful vine, Splendor of Heaven, Blessed Mother of the Son of God, Immaculate Virgin, assist me in this my necessity. O Star of The Sea, help me herein you are my Mother. O Holy Mary, Mother of God, Queen of Heaven and Earth, I humbly beseech thee from the bottom of my heart to succour me in my necessity (make request). There are none that can withstand your power. O show me herein you are my Mother. O Mary, conceived without sin, pray for us who have recourse to thee (3x). Holy Mary I place this cause in your hand (3x). Thank you for your mercy to me and mine. Amen. 3 days and publish, initials SLB

St. Theresa's Prayer

May today there be peace within. May you trust God that you are exactly where you are meant to be. May you not forget the infinite possibilities that are born of faith. May you use those gifts that you have received, and pass on the love that has been given to you. May you be content knowing you are a child of God. Let this presence settle into your bones, and allow your soul the freedom to sing, dance, praise, and love. It is there for each and every one of us. Amen.